# My Reflections With God
*A Straight Line*

Gregory Moore

Copyright © 2017 Gregory Moore
All rights reserved.
Liberation's Publishing LLC ~ West Point Ms. 39773
All scriptures are taken from the Authorized King James
Version of the bible.

ISBN-13: 978-0-9891348-1-1

## Table of Contents

The Notches on the Line .............................. 1

Life .................................................. 9

Death ................................................ 13

God .................................................. 17

Prayers .............................................. 23

Problems ............................................. 31

Anger ................................................ 36

Dreams ............................................... 39

Marriage ............................................. 43

Disobedience ......................................... 51

Spiritual Gifts ...................................... 59

In conclusion ........................................ 67

MATTHEW 7:13-14

"Enter ye in at the strait gate: for wide is the gate, and broad is the way, that leadeth to destruction, and many there be which go in thereat:

Because strait is the gate, and narrow is the way, which leadeth unto life, and few there be that find it."

(KJV)

## The Notches on the Line

When the Lord blesses us to breath and live, we start off on a straight line. All we have to do is follow or walk that line. Because of sin in our heart, we're easily mislead by the devil. We turn a simple line into a tree. See example below.

The notches on the lines are blessings and prayers we asked God for. We should

have gone from point A to point B, but what we end up with is a tree. See the example above.

The notches are still the same our prayers, and the blessings that followed. The difference is it took us longer to get them. Instead of following God's plan we chose to go another way.

The straight line starts to branch off. After putting one branch on the line, we haven't learned our lesson. We go right on to form more branches. Look back at the line. Think back to all the things God has blessed you with. Remember how you prayed for something. Remember how he blessed you in spite of. Now look at the oak tree. Lastly think about the blessings the father gave. This time think about how many detours you took to get the same blessing he was going to give you if you'd stayed on the straight line.

God didn't change a thing. We did. That house, car, wealth, a good peaceful life was all supposed to be ours. What should have been ours in 20 to 30 years was pushed out to 40 to 50 years. Some of us never enjoy our blessings, because of all the detours we took. God has many great fulfilling things in store for us. When we choose to do ungodly things which cause detours off the planned straight line.

Take me for an example, I was going through a bad divorce. My wife and I were fighting over who will get the house and kids. She was teaching my son who was a baby at the time to curse me. She wanted him to call me a bastard. I thought, "I need to let the lawyer know this." It would prove she was unfit to be a parent. There were other things, but I wanted that to be brought out.

God spoke to me that night and said, "GREG YOU REALLY DON'T NEED TO PUT THAT IN THERE. IF YOU DO SHE WILL TELL WHAT YOU DO." My reply to God was, "Yeah, but what she is teaching my son is a lot worse than what I'm doing." God's only reply was, "OKAY."

So, I faxed my lawyer about the cursing my wife was teaching my son and went to bed. The next morning God wakes me up and again starts talking to me about telling my lawyer to bring up the cursing before the judge. God said, "I ASKED YOU NOT TO DO THAT, BUT YOU DID IT. SO YOU WILL BE EMBARRASSED IN FRONT OF THE JUDGE AND ALL WHO ARE IN THE ROOM DURING YOUR TESTIMONY. HER LAWYER WILL BRING UP YOUR MISDEEDS."

To shorten the story, I lost. She got the house and kids. The judge stated my misdeeds were part of the reason for the divorce. My lawyer never mentioned anything about her teaching my son to curse during the trial. He only put it in the papers to her lawyer. This provoked her to bring up my misdeeds during the trial.

Sometime after the smoke had cleared, I did get my house back. I had to buy her out of the deed to the home. God spoke again about what happened. "I TOLD YOU I HAD THIS. YOU ARE BACK IN THE HOUSE, BUT YOU WOULD HAVE BEEN IN YOUR HOUSE WITH YOUR KIDS THE WHOLE TIME YOU WERE GOING THROUGH THE DIVORCE. YOU WOULD HAVE WON THE TRIAL, BUT NO YOU WANTED TO PUT HOW SHE WAS TEACHING YOUR SON TO CURSE. WELL LOOK WHERE IT GOT YOU. YOU WILL GET YOUR KIDS BACK, BUT YOU WILL HAVE TO WAIT NOW.

I was on the straight line, God had

promised me my kids would be back in my life back when I was 24 years old. When I sent my lawyer that fax against the will of the Lord it caused a branch to grow on my lifeline. What could have been me never being without my children has turned into a wait to date 5 years.

I said we could push back our blessings. I did just that push them back. There is no telling how long it may be before God allows me to get my kids back. Listen to God! Stay on the straight line that God has laid out for you. Each detour you cause delays your blessing. Enjoy your blessings. Obey God's commands.

Hebrews 13:17 Obey them that have the rule over you, and submit yourselves: for they watch for your souls, as they that must give account, that they may do it with joy, and not with grief: for that is unprofitable for you. (KJV)

Proverbs 1:8 Obey them that have the rule over you, and submit yourselves: for they watch for your souls, as they that must give account, that they may do it with joy, and not with grief: for that is unprofitable for you. (KJV)

## LIFE

What is LIFE? Or should I say what does life mean to you? Before you read any further I want you to really stop and think about my question. It has different meaning to different people. Life to me is walking, breathing, seeing, and hearing the wonders of God's creation. I love being able to enjoy these things.

It's sad we can get so wrapped up in the cares of the world that we forget to enjoy life. How many of us take time out of our busy schedule to enjoy the wonders God has created. For example have you noticed at how the sun shines bright the first thing in the morning. Its rays shining through the trees ever so soft. Listen to the bristle of the leaves as the wind flows softly through them.

Have you ever looked up at the sky at night and took in the beauty of the stars and planets. Created all of this so we can aw at what he created for us. Yet, we turn a blind eye to it and focus more on worldly things.

The Lord wants us to enjoy life and his creation. So stop and smell the roses. As I've often heard, "Lay all your issues at God's feet so you can enjoy life. "Casting all your care upon him: for he cares for you." (1Peter 5:7) You only have one life. When it's gone, it's gone. Enjoy what God has for you.

Gregory Moore

## Death

Death is something we will all experience. It could be a friend, family, or an acquaintance you just met. At some point in your life you will come face to face with death.

Death should be a time of joy and happiness. We are leaving this world of pain and hardship. We should be happy when our loved ones leave this world. The sorrow should be for our own souls that are remaining here.

I know this may sound like the complete opposite. 2 Corinthians 5:8 "We are confident, I say, and willing rather to be absent from the body, and to be present with the Lord."(KJV)

Sometimes when we pray for healing for ourselves and others we must consider death may be the solution. If it's their time to go don't be upset when the Father calls them home. You don't know how the pain they were going through was too much for them to bear.

I loved my mother dearly. I told her that I asked the Lord to let her live to see my kids grow up to be adults. My mother was in great pain. She had to take several pills to help her deal with pain and prolong her life. She would scream out in pain. Sometimes she would scream out because the medicine had her out of her mind.

I sat with here one day. She screamed out, "YA, please come and get me!" I sat there and listen to her scream over and over again. My heart hurt to hear my mother go through so much pain. I hated to see her not in her right mind. It dawned on me what I had asked God to do. I realized how selfish I was being.

How can anyone say they love someone and watch them suffer and be in pain day in and day out. One day when she was in her right mind I asked her was she tired. She said she was. So I asked the Lord to take her home. About a week later the Father sent his angel to bring my mother home.

I was hurt, but I was glad she wasn't

suffering anymore. She was finally at peace. I miss her dearly. I think about her daily. She was my mother, my friend, and my role model. Romans 6:23 "For the wages of sin is death, but the gift of God is eternal life in Christ Jesus our Lord." (KJV)

John 11:25-26 "Jesus said unto her, I am the resurrection, and the life: he that believeth in me, though he were dead, yet shall he live: 26 And whosoever liveth and believeth in me shall never die. Believest thou this?" (KJV)

## GOD

There are four strong and important questions you should ask yourself about God. Who is he to you? What have you heard about him? What have you read about him? What has he done for you? Some may think these are stupid questions to ask. Some may question, "Where is he going with this?" Let me explain.

There was a time I thought I knew God by going to church every Sunday. I was devout and listen intently to the pastor preach his sermon. Sometimes I even witness the Holy Spirit touch members. They would shout and give God praise. I accepted Christ as my savior at a young age. I knew Jesus Christ died for our sins, and we had to go through him to get to God. God is the Alpha and Omega, and he created the Heavens and Earth. There are so many people that only know God for these acts.

Yes, they go to church. They attend service every Sunday. They listen to the sermon and "amen" with the congregation. They leave church with the joy of knowing they attended service, and God is good. They know the acts of God, but they have no idea who he is or the power he wills. Romans 10:2 states, "For I bear them record that they have a zeal of God, but not according to knowledge."(KJV)

I too was that person. That is until I started to read the bible for myself. When I started to read the Holy Bible for myself I began to see who God is. I began to understand that his will and power is omnipotent. The more I read the more I learned. The more I learned of God's power I grew more afraid of sin. I began to understand why Jesus had to die for ours. I understood why we have to go through Christ to get to God.

It is estimated that God killed 2.8 million people in the old testament for sinning and having wicked ways. Did you know that? The bible of course doesn't speak of all the names of the 2.8 million.

Numbers 21:6 tells how God sent fiery serpents to punish Israel for speaking against him. "The LORD sent fiery serpents among the people and they bit the people; and much people of Israel died."(KJV) Who knows how many died here.

It seemed in the Old Testament God was merciless against sinners. If you read you'll see he was patient, but when the sin became overgrown or rebellious against him or his prophet he killed those. There was no mediator. Hence our need for Christ to die for us. Had he not there would be no us. God's love for us is why he sent Christ. Through Christ we have been equipped with the ability to not be a slave to sin.

Same sex marriage is on the rise. Murders and liars are around every corner.

There are people playing preacher for money and fame. The world seems to be getting worse and worse by the day. Watch the news. We treat sex as if it is a pass time sporting event. Society itself has determined that these things are perfectly fine. Look at TV. Sexual promiscuity of all types is displayed casually every day. It seems as if after government passed the same sex marriage law anything goes.

It's time to know God for yourself. It's not enough to just attend church and say "amen". Time is running out. Christ will be here sooner than you think. You want to be able to know what is happening.

## Prayers

Prayers are a connection we should all have with God. Prayer should be used to thank the Father, or just to have a conversation. You can use this time to ask the Father for something you need or think you need. God is a good God. When you're a child of God he will surely bless you from your prayers.

You need to caution yourself with what you ask for in prayer. As I said before God will surely bless you with what you asked for. Let's take me again for example. I told God if he puts me in the back of the store at my last job I would work there for 20 years. That's all I said to God.

In my praying, I was referring to the office, desk, job. I never exactly said that. Guess what? I was given a receiving manager job at the Back of the Store. It was a stressful job. Unbeknownst to me at the time I was locked in for 20 years. Remember what I said earlier. I would stay 20 years if you put me in the back of the store. Receiving was in the back of the store.

Before I could get another job, I had to put in my 20 years. I had forgotten what I'd asked. That is until I asked him why I couldn't find another job. God reminded me,

"YOU SAID YOU WOULD WORK HERE FOR 20 YEARS IF I PUT YOU IN THE BACK OF THE STORE." I replied, "I meant working back in one of the offices. God simply replied, "THAT'S NOT WHAT YOU SAID. YOU SAID, "IF I PUT YOU IN THE BACK OF THE STORE YOU WOULD WORK HERE FOR 20 YEARS.", AND YOU WILL WORK FOR 20 YEARS BEFORE YOU CAN LEAVE." I said, "Okay."

When my 20 years were up the Father did bless me to leave. It was a better job and a lot less stressful. When you pray make sure you don't leave anything out. Don't ever say, "The Lord knows what I meant." No, the Lord knows what you asked for. Never limit what you pray for.

Here's another example. I'd been praying for financial wealth for months. I asked the Lord for 10 million dollars so I could pay off all my bills. I wanted to take care of my parents. I wanted to pay off my true friend's debt, and give them some money. I would pay off close family members bills and give them some money.

I prayed for months and months for the same thing. One night I said, "Well God hasn't answered me or blessed me with the money yet." I decided to ask for a smaller amount. I began to pray again asking for financial wealth. I first said, "Please bless me with 5 million." Then I reasoned no, maybe if I take it down some more he would surely bless me. This is all going through my mind as I'm praying. I thought again, "Well maybe if I ask for 2.5 million he would answer my prayer and I would be wealthy." So, I said my prayer and asked him for the 2.5 million in financial wealth.

As soon as I finished my prayer the Farther said, "WHY DID YOU CHANGE AND ASK FOR LESS?" I said, "Well Father I thought I was asking for too much and you wouldn't give it to me." God replied, "SO YOU THOUGHT I WOULDN'T BLESS YOU WITH 10 MILLION SO YOU WENT FOR LESS. OKAY, 2.5 MILLION IT IS. THERE IS NO TAKE BACKS. I quickly replied, "Wait Father..." He said, "NO, YOU DON'T TRUST ME TO BLESS YOU WITH 10 SO YOU ASKED FOR LESS."

I laid in bed thinking about what I had done. I cut my blessing by doing two things in my prayer. First I limited my blessing by asking for a lesser amount. Second I didn't have faith enough to trust the Lord that he would answer my prayer. Our faith must match our prayer. What I mean is if you have the heart and the faith to ask for it, why turn weak or turn away from the faith that will get it for you. We must stay strong and have an unshakeable faith.

Mark 11:24 Therefore I say unto you, what things so ever ye desire, when ye pray, believe that ye receive them, and ye shall have them. (KJV)

Matthew 21:22 "And whatever you ask in prayer, you will receive if you have faith. (KJV)

John 15:7 "If ye abide in me, and my words abide in you, ye shall ask what ye will, and it shall be done unto you." (KJV)

Gregory Moore

## Problems

We all have problems. Some are big, some are small, but all are problems. They are part of life we all have them. Money problems, job problems, transportation problems, children, medical you name it. I have learned a problem is not a problem until you make it a problem. Let me give you an example.

We all get up and do our daily task working, cooking whatever. On a good day you have no worries. At that moment there is no thought of anything going wrong, therefore you haven't labeled anything as a problem. Do you see where I'm going with this? A problem doesn't become a problem until it is named so. That is all a problem really is. Something we put a name to. If we stop putting a name on it, and focus more on getting to know God, trusting in his word, problem would not come up.

Some of what we call problem are test. A test is something we deserve. It could be something I am going through for disobeying God. Just think of all the energy we spend by worrying, when all we need to do is turn it over to God. Have faith that he will fix it.

It's hard for us to do that. We'll sit around and worry. Some people have even killed themselves over their problems, failing God's test. I sometimes sit down and think what could have been so bad they had to take their life? I question if they ever knew God. To know God is to know of his love for you and all mankind.

We should never put a name on anything that brings sadness or despair to us. 1 Timothy 1:7 says, "For God hath not given us the spirit of fear; but of power, and of love, and of a sound mind." (KJV) We bring sadness and fear into our own lives.

While writing this I did some soul searching. I had fear in my heart concerning my bills. I didn't call paying my bills a problem, but I did fear the phone ringing. I hated looking in the mail box. I even feared that on my returning home from work I would see a notice on my front door.

Trust and faith, these two words we cannot do without. As much as I love God I still fell short. I remember in the bible where Peter had the same test. Matthew 14:26-33 When the disciples saw Him walking on the sea, they were terrified, and said, "It is a ghost!" And they cried out in fear. 27 But immediately Jesus spoke to them, saying, "Take courage, it is I; do not be afraid."

28 Peter said to Him, "Lord, if it is You, command me to come to You on the water." 29 And He said, "Come!" And Peter got out of the boat, and walked on the water and came toward Jesus. 30But seeing the wind, he became frightened, and beginning to sink, he cried out, "Lord, save me!" 31 Immediately Jesus stretched out His hand and took hold of him, and said to him, "You of little faith, why did you doubt?" 32 When

they got into the boat, the wind stopped. 33 And those who were in the boat worshiped Him, saying, "You are certainly God's Son!"

Peter's request to walk on water is no different than us asking for cars, houses, and money any of our heart desire. Whenever it gets hard we fear. We start to doubt. Matthew 21: 21-22 "And Jesus answered and said to them, "Truly I say to you, if you have faith and do not doubt, you will not only do what was done to the fig tree, but even if you say to this mountain, 'Be taken up and cast into the sea,' it will happen. 22 "And all things you ask in prayer, believing, you will receive."

## Anger

Anger is an emotion that we have. Even Jesus got angry. Ephesians 4:26 "Be ye angry, and sin not: let not the sun go down upon your wrath:"(KJV) When dealing with anger the most important thing to decipher is why.

We are all children of God. We will face many situations that can and will bring about anger. It is the way we deal with this anger that we must consider. For instance when someone lies on you view it for what it is. It is a lie. It is an untruth. Someone is trying to bring you down. Just know what is happening. There are people out there that hate happy people. They will do their best to make you angry.

Keep in mind it is the devil's job to get you off course. A person will say and do anything to get a reaction out of you. As soon as you respond in anger the first thing out of their mouth is, "You must not be who you say you are. You must not be as close to God as you say."

What if what they say is true? The truth is the truth own it. You have to face your truths and move on with your life. The more you let anger consume you the more people will be against you.

If someone wronged you asked God for

strength. This is the biggest cause for anger. As we grow in God we must remember that there are people that will hurt you for no reason. We have to continue to pray the Lord's prayer,

"After this manner therefore pray ye: Our Father which art in heaven, Hallowed be thy name. 10 Thy kingdom come. Thy will be done in earth, as it is in heaven. 11 Give us this day our daily bread. 12 And forgive us our debts, as we forgive our debtors. 13 And lead us not into temptation, but deliver us from evil: For thine is the kingdom, and the power, and the glory, forever. Amen. 14For if ye forgive men their trespasses, your heavenly Father will also forgive you: 15 But if ye forgive not men their trespasses, neither will your Father forgive your trespasses" (KJV)

## Dreams

The LORD blesses us with 12 hrs sometimes more, of daylight. At night we reset our bodies and mind. During that time we sometimes dream. Your dream could be about anything. The bible has a story about Joseph. He was an interpreter of dreams. In knowing this we know our dreams have meaning.

I read somewhere once about a man who made a deal with the devil in his dream. This scared me, because I didn't know the devil would attack us when we were sleep. I knew he could and would during day hours, but never at night while we rested.

After reading the story it really upset me. How could this be? We are resting after a hard day of activities and he comes to attack. I just couldn't understand how God allows him to come to us while we are asleep.

God soon brought this to my mind, "The devil has no set time to call upon you. Prayer is the key, and a man who is prayed up is a man who will be defended by me. I knew then how this could happen to the man in the story.

He didn't have a strong relationship with God and he wasn't prayed up. You should pray day and night. We all need protection even when we're sleeping. You don't know when he will call on you.

I had a powerful dream last night. I was told, "Satan will attack you whenever he can." In my dream I was fighting Satan. In the middle of us fighting God gave me a sword. Satan had a staff. I mean it was a battle. Satan would turn into sand and move from place to place as we defended ourselves against each other.

A thought came to me that this was Satan and what would happen if I lost to him. I could feel fear trying to take over me. I wouldn't let it, because my faith in God is stronger than fear. My faith in God made me strong.

As Satan put his staff up to block my

sword I struck it with all of my weight breaking it and defeating him. I don't know the meaning of the dream, but when I woke up a weight had lifted off of me.

This helped me to know that Satan will attack you in your sleep. I used to think this wasn't possible. I was wrong. I'm so glad God showed me and gave me the strength to win the fight.

This has helped me to stay with my daily talks with God before I go to sleep as well as saying my prayers.

## Marriage

The bible speaks highly of marriage, and tells us it is a good thing in the eye of the LORD. Today's world treats marriage as a joke. There's an estimate 93,750 divorces a year in the United States. If we took marriage seriously there would be far less or none at all.

Marriage is hard work. I used to call it my second job. It shouldn't be considered as a second job. God didn't mean it to be that way. Marriage should be a happy union between a man and woman who love and respect each other. This love and respect should last until death. Now days you're lucky if it last a year. What does that say about how the world views marriage?

Then there's the desire to play house before getting marriage. It's a sin in God's eyes. If you feel he or she is worthy to live with and have sex with shouldn't they be worthy of the title of husband or wife? I have heard people say I want to test drive my car before I buy it. Well, people are not cars, and sex shouldn't be the only basis for a good marriage. Love, respect, and God will cover all your needs in your marriage. God should be first and second your love for God. Your love and respect for each other will be key. Without this your marriage will be a tough road to travel. You will end up a part of that 93,750 divorces filed.

Years ago I was part of that 93,750. I didn't have all 4 in my first marriage. I only had one of them, and that road was one of the toughest I had ever traveled. I hated to come home. Each day I left my paying job to go home to another job at home. It got so bad I finally said, "Father I give up, but I will stay married and unhappy to keep my kids with me." His only response, "REALLY!!" Until this moment he had been silent on the matter. Two days later my wife asked for a divorce. A week later I was served with divorce papers.

There was a weight off of my shoulder and some joy in my heart. I was tired of being unhappy. I was tired of dealing with the problems in my marriage. After the divorce was finalized I said words I often heard people say, "Once is good enough for me never again." During the course of my single life I rebuilt my relationship with God. He spoke to me, "GREG IF YOU HADN'T GOTTEN MARRIED WHERE WOULD YOU BE?" I said, "In the house my dad gave me." He replied, "OKAY, WOULD YOU HAVE FIXED IT UP ANY OR LEFT IT AS IT WAS?" I said, "I would have worked on it." His reply was, "AND YOU WOULDN'T HAVE BUILT A NEW HOME RIGHT?" I replied, "No. I would still be living in my great grandmother's house." "WHAT ABOUT YOUR KIDS? WOULD YOU HAVE KNOWN THEM OR TRIED TO ADOPT KIDS IF YOU HADN'T GOTTEN MARRIED? NO. SO STOP LOOKING AT THIS AS A BAD

THING."

After God finished bringing all that back to my attention, all the things I allowed to go on in my marriage, I realized he was preparing me for something better. I took a step back and looked back on all that had happened. I started thanking him for the steps he took me through. I was grateful for where I was. God had given me a new home for my family.

I learned somethings over the course if time that I believe sabotages the success of marriage from the beginning. First there is the issue of fidelity. Many enter into marriage being unfaithful. Second, there's the issue of money. Some people get married wanting someone to take care of them financially. Some people enter marriage with lack of money or too much debt. It's not discussed beforehand. Third, there's the issue of children. A parents love for their child can be exploited. It can be used to make someone get married. Some men and women don't want to see another person raising their children. These three things seem to be the most prominent.

What signs did God show you? How did he try and get you to see you were making a bad decision in marrying? Was it in the form of a dream? Did your friends and family try to warn you? Did you have bad dreams of the one you were with? In my case, I lost the voice of God. He stopped talking to me. When you have a good relationship with God, he tells you in many ways why this person isn't for you. When you ignore him, you cannot blame him for being silent afterwards.

Sometimes the fear of being alone is a big factor in marrying. I understand being alone day in and day out can and will get lonely. There are things you can do while waiting on your mate. Build your relationship with God. Study the bible. Talk to God about it. He loves for us talk to him. He's our father. Finding a hobby to pass the time is a great thing also.

Usually over the course of getting closer to God, he'll give you a hobby. These hobbies turn out to be very lucrative. My hobbies are building furniture. This turned out to be very lucrative. I love working in my yard. I watch TV. Even though I wasn't looking for anything serious, I went on dates. Hanging out with others, especially friends and family made for a good time.

## Disobedience

God calls us disobedient when we break his commandments, or when we go against something he told us to do. As a child of God, we should know better, but as human beings we want what we want. We spend so much time crying and complaining asking, "Why do bad things keep happening to me?" Why am I having such a hard time? I want you to stop saying all that. Look back before everything went bad and think. Did God warn you? Did he show you another way to handle the situation?

I am willing to bet that he did. You didn't listen, or you let the devil tell you something different all together. God is not going to make us listen to him. He's not going to make us follow him. Everything we do is by choice. When the blessings don't come the way that you expected it's all on you. So, when you're lying in bed, in your car, on a bench, or the street and wonder how you got there remember you got you there. Most of the time it's because of the choices you made. You made the choice to disobey God.

The devil loves when our patience is short. We want relief right now. God builds things by plan. So the house it seems as if it is taking you forever to get is really being put together by God's plan. The financial wealth you're waiting on. It seems as if it is delayed. It's not. These things and more are coming, but we have to have patience and be obedient.

The devil will come and show you what seems like an easier way. What is it really? It's a delay. You are moving off your straight line. You are moving away from God's plans to get you to your destination. God's plans have lessons that we learn along the path. These lessons allow us to be able to accept and hold on to our blessing. The devil gives things quick, but you lose it fast.

You will receive every blessing God has for you. You must stay obedient and have patience. There may be times when you don't know when or how you are going to pay your bills or get food. I am a living witness that if you keep your faith, walk in obedience, and be patient you will have an answer.

God knows your struggles. You don't have to fix them alone. Don't put God on a shelf and start going about making decisions for yourselves. He will let you. He will not budge on your behalf. When you get tired because nothing is working then God will ask you, "Are you ready for me to handle this now?"

God is ready, and waiting for us to turn to him for help and guidance. We forget who's in charge of our life. God will let you believe that until you hit a brick wall. Your straight line has become a crocked path.

Being obedient to God may seem hard.

It can be done. Stay in his word. Read your bible daily. Take time out of each day and talk to him. Ask him questions about what you read in the bible. Pray daily and nightly, throughout the day, even while you're driving.

God wants to build strong a relationship with you. Once you do you'll find out that being obedient isn't that hard at all.

While I was going through my divorce the judge awarded my wife the kids and house. I had to move in with my parents. I didn't like this arrangement at all. I was 45 years old, and I was living back at home with my parents. They lived in a three bedroom one bath home. When the kids would come to visit it was difficult. It was hard for six people living in a small home like that.

I had been on my own for 27 years. Now I was back living in my parents' home with their rules. It made me feel like less than a man. So, I moved out. I took on another job. This freed up my 401K. I wanted to use it. God told me not to. He even sent me a warning through my mother. I was so impatient. I wanted to get away from my parents' home and their rules. I spent my 401K on a new place. I started doing worldly thing in addition to this. Before I knew it I had spent all my 401K.

After I had spent the last of my 401K judgement came down on me. I had to buy my ex-wife out of our house. I had no money. This lead to me having to borrow money that I wasn't able to pay back. With all the money coming out of my check it was a struggle to pay my mortgage, keep gas in my car, and food on the table.

All this happened because I was disobedient. As I said before God forgives us, but we reap what we sow.

## Spiritual Gifts

We're all blessed with a gift. If you sing and never had to have a lesson that's a gift. Any talent or talents you have God blessed you with them. My advice for you is, use them. If you don't use them as sure as he blessed you with them he will take them away.

We often find ways not to use our blessings. "I work too much to join the church choir. I don't have time to build that house." Whatever your excuse is. Let me tell you about my experience.

The Lord told me how to build a part they now use on a weedeater. I said, "Lord who is going to listen to a black boy from Mississippi.
Besides I know someone else has already come up with the idea." Well someone else did come up with the idea 3 years later. Look at how popular weedeaters are.

Do you know how rich I could have been if I had just listen and followed through with the gift God had given me? Now I do what he tells me.

Before I started building furniture I was struggling to make ends meet. At times I didn't have enough money to buy myself food to eat. I would pray, "Father please help me. Please bless me financially so I can pay my home off and live comfortably." God didn't reply back right away. Then one day I was at work and I saw a stack of boards in the middle of the floor. So I asked, "What are you going to do with them?" One of the guys replied, "We're going to throw them away." I looked at them and said, "That's some good wood to be throwing away." As I looked closer at the wood the Lord showed me an image of a cedar chest in my mind. He then laid out the plans on how this could be my extra income. Me being me I questioned God on this chest building plan.

I rushed home from work with about eight boards and went to work on building the chest God showed me. Well the first one was a mess. It was four feet long, thirty inches tall, and twenty-four inches wide. It

was way too big to call a chest. It looked more like a storage box for tools.

I turned to God and said, "This isn't going to work. I'm not a carpenter, and I haven't built anything before with wood." His response to me was, "SLOW DOWN AND THINK ABOUT WHAT YOU ARE ABOUT TO BUILD. I WANT TO YOU TO PUT YOUR HEART INTO WHAT YOU ARE ABOUT TO BUILD."

So I did as he asked. I took my time. I looked at my mother's old cedar chest. I

took measurements. As I worked on the chest I cleared my mind and allowed God to show me how to cut and piece together the chest.

When I was done I was knocked off my feet at how nice it turned out. Now keep in mind I had no wood working training. The only tools I had were a hammer and a skill saw (see above). As a matter of fact I was afraid of the skill saw. I had only used one a couple of times when I was a teenager in $8^{th}$ grade.

The Lord showed me how to build the chest and he kept showing me. He should me how these chest would help me financially. I had to make the next chest even better. If I was going to sell them I had to perfect it.

My day job started ordering overtime. With that extra money I started buying the things I needed to build a better chest. I purchased wood stain, a cordless drill, and polyurethane to give it a shine. Once I had purchased everything I needed I started telling people about my side job. I let them know I build chests and asked them if they'd like to purchase one.

I had two ladies at work to order one from me. One of the ladies even asked me to build her a 4x4 corner table to serve food on.

I started getting orders and the money I was receiving was helping me out just as God had shown me.

Over the course of time I stopped building furniture for about 9 months to a year. During that time I had gotten married with the marriage came more challenges. Once again I found myself asking God for help. His response to me was, "GREG, YOU AND PAULA ARE STRUGGLING BECAUSE YOU WANT TO. I TOLD YOU TO BUILD FURNITURE AND TO PUBLISH THE BOOK. I EVEN TOLD PAULA WHAT TO DO. SO I DON'T KNOW WHAT MORE YOU WANT."

After he said that I told my wife we have to do what he has said to do. Our money was tight so I borrowed money from my 401k. I picked up supplies and started back building furniture. I made a down payment to my now publisher who I had meet three weeks earlier.

## In conclusion

These are just a few of my reflections with God. I wanted to share with you the importance of relationship with him. He desires to be an active part of our everyday life. God will grow and expand you in so many ways.

As I said earlier in the book God gave me a gift of building furniture. He instructed me to complete this book that you are reading now. I pray it has done what God intended for it to do.

Here are pictures of my work you. You can see how far I have come. This book and these pieces of furniture are all here because of my relationship with God. They are here because of my faith. Be blessed and look for more to come!

These are the tools I've added to my set.

My Reflections with God ... A Straight Line

# Gregory Moore

# My Reflections with God ... A Straight Line

Gregory Moore

My Reflections with God ... A Straight Line

Gregory Moore

www.ingramcontent.com/pod-product-compliance
Lightning Source LLC
Chambersburg PA
CBHW052029290426
44112CB00014B/2434